This is the story about the wonderful things that can happen when people love God and each other. It's the story of Ruth, and you can read it in the Bible.

Long ago in the land of Moab lived a girl
named Ruth. When she was old enough to be married,
her parents arranged for her to marry Mahlon,
a young man from Bethlehem in the land of Judah.
He, his mother and father and brother had moved
to Moab during a great famine in Judah when no one
had enough to eat.

Ruth and her parents must have liked Mahlon
very much, even though Mahlon was a foreigner.
He didn't have the freedom of other young men
in Moab because in those days foreigners
in a country were considered outsiders
and could not do many things.

The people in Moab worshiped many different gods.
But Ruth learned about the one God from Mahlon
and his mother, Naomi. Through them,
Ruth came to trust God's goodness and love.

In a few years Mahlon, as well as his father
and brother, had died. Only Naomi was left
of the family from Bethlehem. Usually young women
returned to their mothers' homes if their husbands died.
But Ruth and her sister-in-law Orpah loved Naomi
and stayed with her. When the famine was over
in the land of Judah and Naomi decided
to return home, they wanted to go with her.

They started out together. But Naomi thought
the young women would be happier in their own country.
"Return each of you to your own mother's house,"
she said. "And may God be as kind to you as you
have been to my sons and me."

Orpah kissed Naomi and turned back. But Ruth wouldn't go.

It wasn't easy to be leaving her parents, friends, and her own country. It wouldn't be easy to live as a foreigner in Bethlehem. But Ruth loved Naomi dearly. And she loved God, whom the people in the land of Judah knew and worshiped.

So hugging Naomi, Ruth said, "I'm not going back. Wherever you go I will go. Wherever you live I will live. Your people will be my people. And your God will be my God."

Then Ruth and Naomi went on together. They arrived in Bethlehem at the beginning of barley harvest.

In those days it was hard for women alone to earn a living. But Ruth saw reapers in the grain fields outside Bethlehem. They were cutting barley stalks and gathering them. Later, bread could be made from the grain in the stalks. Ruth saw this was a way to get food for Naomi and herself.

"I'm going to the fields," Ruth told Naomi. "If someone will let me, I'll pick up stalks of barley that the reapers drop."

"Go, my daughter," Naomi encouraged her.

Early the next morning Ruth went to the barley fields. As she walked along the dewy path, she probably thought about what lay ahead. Ruth was a foreigner in Bethlehem. No one had to let her work in his field. No one had to give her anything. They might even harm her. But Ruth had not been afraid to leave her home in Moab, and she was not afraid now.

Listening to God, she went straight to the man in charge of one of the groups of workers. "May I follow your reapers and pick up the stalks that they drop?" she asked.

"Go right ahead," the man answered.

Ruth worked all morning under the blazing sun. After a while she was so hot and tired that she sat down to rest in a little shelter in the field.

Just then Boaz, the owner of that field, came to see how his reapers were getting along.

He noticed Ruth right away.

"Who is that in our shelter?" he asked.

"She's the young Moabitess who came back
with Naomi," the man answered. "She asked if she
could pick up the stalks our reapers drop. She
works hard. This is the first time she has rested
since she began."

Boaz walked over to Ruth. "Stay here with my people," he said. "You'll be safe with them. I've told them not to bother you. And when you're thirsty, drink from the jars that my men have filled."

Ruth bowed clear to the ground before him. "Why are you so kind to me?" she asked. "I'm a foreigner in your land."

Boaz smiled. "I've been told all you've done for Naomi. Everyone in Bethlehem knows how you left your parents and your own country to come to a people and place you didn't know before. God will reward you. God in whom you trust will surely repay your goodness."

Boaz invited Ruth to share his reapers' noonday meal. And when she went back to work, he told the workers to drop some stalks on purpose so that Ruth would have plenty.

Ruth worked in the field of Boaz until evening.
It was hot, hard work. But she had almost a bushel
of barley to take home, besides some food she
had saved from her lunch for Naomi.

"Such richness!" Naomi cried when she saw what Ruth brought home. "Where did you work?"

"In the field of Boaz," Ruth replied. 'He's very kind. He even invited me to share his reapers' noonday meal."

"Blessed be God and His kindness!" Naomi said happily. "Boaz is one of my husband's nearest relatives. He's an important man in Bethlehem and well liked."

"He wants me to work in his field till harvest is over," Ruth said.

"Good!" Naomi exclaimed. "No harm will come to you there."

When harvesting was done and the barley was cut and gathered, Naomi said to Ruth, "My daughter, I'd like to see you happily married, in a home of your own. Listen carefully to what I want you to do."

That night, as Naomi had told her, Ruth went to see Boaz. He was where the grain was being separated from the stalks of barley.

"You are a near relative," Ruth said to him.
"Please spread your robe over me." In those days
that meant Ruth was asking Boaz to marry her.

"God bless you, my dear," Boaz cried. "I would
like nothing better. You are a fine young woman.
All Bethlehem knows that! But there is a man who
is a closer relative to you than I am. According
to the ancient law, he must be asked first.
I will see him in the morning."

Early the next day Boaz went to the city gate,
which was a place of business. "Ho, friend," Boaz
called when he found the other man. "Sit down."

Then Boaz invited ten of the leaders of Bethlehem to be witnesses to hear what they would say.

"Naomi has come home from the land of Moab," Boaz began. "She wants to sell a plot of ground that belonged to her husband and their sons. According to the ancient law, as their nearest relative, you can buy it."

"I'll buy it," the man answered instantly.

"According to the ancient law," Boaz continued, "when you buy the ground you must also marry Ruth."

"Oh," said the other man. "I can't do that."

"Then I shall marry Ruth," said Boaz, and the ten men whom he had invited to hear what was said declared, "We are witnesses."

So Ruth the Moabitess married Boaz of Bethlehem. And they shared their home and happiness with Naomi. Now Ruth was no longer a poor stranger in Bethlehem in the land of Judah. She was the loved and loving wife of a good and kind man.

After a while, a son was born to Ruth and Boaz. He was to be the grandfather of David, who defeated Goliath and became the favorite king of Israel. Ruth was also a many-times great-grandmother of Jesus.